Boolean String Basics for Recruiters

By: Jonathan Kidder

'Thank you to Irina Shamaeva and Dean Da Costa for lighting a path and giving direction to other Sourcers."

Legal Disclaimer

Table of Contents

A Beginner's Guide to Boolean Strings

Back when I first started my recruiting career thing's we're quite as defined within the searching space. A lot of what I learned about Boolean and Talent Sourcing we're self-taught from online resources.

Around 2014 my manager encouraged the team to attend SourceCon and at the time I was not aware of this conference but highly looked forward to attending.

During the event I was able to see Dean, Irina, and Shally present on the topics of talent sourcing and Boolean search. It truly was a light bulb moment for me and the team. It really helped me to push myself to the next level. From that moment on the spark was lit for me to learn as much about Boolean string and its benefits for finding great talent online. From that moment on I was hooked on learning about talent sourcing. In 2015, I started the blog

WizardSourcer.com as resource for other Recruiters and Talent Sourcers. Present day, WizardSourcer.com has become one of the most visited and recommend recruiting sites online!

[Picture from SourceCon 2014 hosted by Jeremy Roberts]

I wrote this book as a guide for Recruiters and Talent Sourcers. Whether you've recently started or have some experience in the field. I wanted to create a guide that will walk you through understanding the basics to creating a great Boolean string.

Talent Sourcing comes down to finding talent and in order to do that it first starts with creating a search.
Search engines use Boolean logic to make this happen. This book will help you find resumes, profiles, directory lists, company intel, and much more online!

About Jonathan Kidder

Jonathan Kidder, AKA the "WizardSourcer," is a top-ranked technical talent sourcing recruiter, staffing expert, and corporate trainer who assists organizations of all sizes in identifying and attracting top talent.

A wizard at harnessing the power of social networking, Boolean strings, search aggregators, deep web searching, scrapers, and other advanced technology tricks and tools. In 2015, he founded a recruiting blog called WizardSourcer, which has become one of the leading knowledge resources for recruiters online.

His mission is simple: To help Recruiters and Talent Sourcers learn about Boolean search strings.

With nearly a decade of full-cycle recruiting and sourcing experience under his belt, he has worked in talent sourcing and recruiting with companies including Amazon, Vista Outdoor, CA Technologies, American Express, and many others.

Throughout his career as a sourcing leader, he has pursued continuous learning to stay current on the latest sourcing trends and to help clients across industries maximize the use of high-tech recruiting tools ranging from browser extensions to AI automation.

After earning a bachelor's in business from Bethel University in Saint Paul, Minnesota, Jonathan launched his sourcing career at Allegis Global Solutions, one of the world's largest RPO staffing companies.

At Allegis, Jonathan discovered the power of social media as a recruiting tool. This inspired him to develop and implement a proprietary employer branding EVP and recruitment marketing plan that could be used with any client to attract the world's best available talent.

A sought-after speaker and mentor, Jonathan has trained teams around the globe on best practices for sourcing and recruiting top talent. One of the industry's emerging go-to resources on recruiting expertise in the 21st century, he writes regularly on the latest recruiting trends for his own top-ranked blog at WizardSourcer in addition to being a contributing writer for AI recruiting platform Hiretual and Recruitingblogs.com.

Jonathan is the author of 8 published recruiting books all available on Amazon. He currently lives in Minneapolis with his wife and adopted golden doodle dogs Dolly & Henry.

Chapter 1: Boolean Defined:

Boolean is the foundation to conducting a search online. When creating a search string you are implying the principles of [OR, AND, NOT]. Maybe without you realizing this many Search Engines like Google, Bing, Duckduckgo use these principles to help the user find what they are looking for online.

In 1854, a mathematician named George Boole published "The Laws of Thought" which contains Boolean algebra. Boolean logic is credited with creating the foundation of the information age. This basic logic has been the construct of how modern people find things online.

Searching has been simplified and modernized on search engines but the same principles can be used to narrow down an exact search. While searching has become straightforward there are still billions of searchable websites available online. This can become quite a task to search through content online to find what you are looking for. Many of what Recruiters and Sourcers are looking for might not be highly ranked within a search engine's results as well.

Searches have been convoluted with PPC advertisements and SEO rankings. Bloggers, Web Developers, and SEO specialists work on the back end to drive results to their pages.

Recruiters need to understand the basics of Boolean logic to effectively find resumes, profiles, directories, lists, company intelligence, company org's and much more online. You will need to be able to peel back search results to find exactly what you are looking for.

Within this book, I will define Boolean, showcase the benefits, give examples on creating searches, and ultimately turn you (the reader) into a more effective "cyber sleuth" Boolean searcher. Talent Sourcing tasks take most a recruiter's day. Understanding Boolean logic and terminology will help advance your knowledge and will benefit you greatly in your recruiting career.

Chapter 2: Search Engines Explained

A search engine is designed to help an internet user search and find web pages. Once you complete a search the results page represents links, pages, images, videos, and files. Search engines maintain results by using algorithms and web crawlers to help showcase the most relevant page results. Content or pages not available on a search engine can still be found on the Deep Web. You can however access those pages using a TOR Browser.

Below I will walk through the [3] most widely used search engines. Note, each one has different rules and search terminology.

Google:
Word order does matter. Google Ranks the first keywords in higher order.
- Has a maximum of 32 keywords in each search.
- [AND] does not work within a search instead use a space.
- Below are Google's Operators and Modifiers:
    - ()
    - ""

- NOT –
- OR |

Searching is a major part of any recruiter's job, and luckily, Google makes it quite easy to find what you're looking for, so long as you go beyond the basic word search option. Once you learn Google's advanced search operators, you can find exactly what you need in far less time. The key is knowing which to use and when.

Here's a look at the top Google Search Operators that recruiters can use when sourcing for candidates:

site:example.com

This is one of the most basic search operators you can use, and it will certainly come in handy. This will produce two pieces of information: the list of pages in the site's index and the number of pages in the site's index.

site:example.com/folder

Want to dive deeper into a site's sub-folder, like "/blog"? This is the search operator to use. Add it to the end of any root domain and you'll soon have all the info you need.

site:sub.example.com

If you want to get down into a site's sub-domains, this search operator is another good one to use.

site:example.com inurl:www

This operator can help you find a domain's sub-domain.

Add a [-] to exclude options

If you add a "-" before the search operator of number four, you'll be able to tell Google to find anything except that specific text. In this case, you can use it in front of "inurl:www" to find any indexed URLs for that site that don't have the "www" sub-domain, as in: site:example.com -inurl:www

Chain operators to get more done

Most operators can be chained, which means you can get to very specific information just by combining different operators to produce the search you want to perform. For example: site:example.com -inurl:www -inurl:dev -inurl:shop.

site:example.com inurl:https

If you want to find any secure pages on a site, you can use this operator.

site:example.com inurl:param

If you're worried about pagination, search sorts, or something else, using "inurl" and a parameter to track down pages is handy.

site:example.com -inurl:param

This operator allows you to know all sorts of things, like how many pages are being indexed for a specific website without sorts.

site:example.com text goes here

You can also combine the "site" operator with a plain text query. This means you'll be able to search a page's entire content for certain or relevant text. Google will try to match all the terms you put in, but they may be separated or the search may only return certain terms.

site:example.com "text goes here"

If you want an exact match to the text you put in, simply surround your text with quotation marks and Google will look for an exact match. This is great for tracking down specific details.

site:example.com/folder "text goes here"

You can also use the above operator to check for content within a specific folder, whether you're looking for an exact match (with quotations) or just any relevant results (without quotations).

site:example.com this OR that

Google does allow you to use "OR" in your queries if you are looking for something specific. If you don't know what exact term you're looking for out of a couple options, this operator could be very useful.

site:example.com "top * ways"

The asterisk acts as a wildcard, allowing you to look for unknown text.

site:example.com "top 7..10 ways"

If you have a number range in mind for a search, you can always search using X...Y. It will return anything within the range of X to Y.

Pro tip you can search graduations dates using this operator function i.e. > 2009..2011

site:example.com intitle:"text goes here"

When you search for something using the "intitle" operator, it will only return text that's within <TITLE> tags.

site:example.com intitle:"text * here"

You can vary the last few operators to use "intitle:"

intitle:"text goes here"
This "intitle" search returns matching queries from across the entire web.

"text goes here" -site:example.com

This operator allows you to find text on any site, while excluding a certain domain. It could be useful if you're trying to find a company or candidate's info outside of their main website or profile.

site:example.com filetype:pdf

If you're looking for something of a specific file type, using the "filetype" search operator is the way to go. For instance, this one allows you to find all PDFs on a given domain, but you could search for other formats, too.

Bing:

- By default, all searches are AND searches.

- You must capitalize the NOT and OR operators. Otherwise, Bing will ignore them as stop words, which are commonly occurring words and numbers that are omitted to speed a full-text search.

- Stop words and all punctuation marks, except for the symbols noted in this topic, are ignored unless they are surrounded by quotation marks or preceded by the + symbol.

- Only the first 10 terms are used to get search results.

- Because OR is the operator with lowest precedence, enclose OR terms in parentheses when combined with other operators in a search.

- Below are Bings Operators and Modifiers:
  - ()
  - ""
  - NOT –
  - + [Finds web pages that contain all the terms that are preceded by the + symbol. Also allows you to include terms that are usually ignored.]
  - AND &
  - OR |

DuckDuckgo:
- cats dogs [Results about cats or dogs]

- "cats and dogs" [Results for exact term "cats and dogs". If no results are found, we'll try to show related results.]

- cats -dogs [Fewer dogs in results]

- cats +dogs [More dogs in results cats]

- cats filetype:pdf [PDF docs about cats. Supported file types: pdf, doc(x), xls(x), ppt(x), html]

- dogs site:example.com [Pages about dogs from example.com]

- cats -site:example.com [Pages about cats, excluding example.com]

- intitle:dogs [Page title includes the word "dogs"]

- inurl:cats [Page url includes the word "cats"]

Chapter 3: Modifiers and Operators

Boolean logic is the foundation of AND OR NOT (). This is the most basic way to create a Boolean string. You will need to understand each individual one and why it's important for getting search results.

" "	Quotes find the exact words in a phrase.
()	Finds or excludes webpages that contain a group of words.
AND or [SPACE]	Finds web pages that contain all the terms or phrases. Google uses [SPACE] instead of AND in searches.

NOT or –	Excludes web pages that contain a term or phrase. Most search engines use [-] only within the search.
OR or |	Finds web pages that contain either of the terms or phrases.
*	Asterisk helps suggest and gives every variation within a search term. For example [Contact me at this event] versus [contact me **]

List of Advanced Search Operators:

[site:] search also known as xraying helps you search the entire website domain for keywords.

Some examples include:

site:github.com

site:linkedin.com
site:facebook.com
site:twitter.com
site:instagram.com

[inurl:] searching for URL pages of a website.

[intitle:] searching the titles of a web page.
[filetype:] searching for different file type formats. For example, TXT, PDF, CSV, or XLSX files.

filetype:(pdf OR doc OR docx OR rtf)

[relate:] searching for websites that are similar within a search.

related:reddit.com will suggest other sites like Twitch or StumbleUpon.

[intext:] searching for keywords in the text of a website.

Chapter 4: Defining Searchable Terms

In this chapter, we'll go through synonym and antonym examples. There's many different types of keyword terms or phrases that can change up a search.

For example, searching the term Apple might give you back results of fruit, the company name, or even the term Big Apple. So, consider the phrasing and word placement when constructing a string.

You can use inurl: and intitle: when adding these below terms to your Boolean string.

Note: Missed spelled words can also impact a result. For example, a person might miss spell resume incorrectly. So, you could even play around with miss spelling words on profiles or resumes.

Searching for Directory:
Our team
Meet our team
List
Attendees
Event
Agenda

Archive
Inventory
Group
Member List
Management Team

Searching for Events:
Attendees
Conference
Virtual Event

Searching for Alumni:
Alumni
Graduates
Post graduates
Networking

Searching for Diversity:
Minority owned
Women led
Women in tech
Women owned
African american
Black women
Latin X

Searching for College or Universities:
Graduating
Graduated
Completed masters
Degree

Computer science
Completed school

Searching for Resumes:
Portfolio
Resume
CV
Curriculum Vitae
Bio
Synopsis

Make sure to research additional phrases or keywords when creating your Boolean string.

Here's a Boolean Strings Cheat Sheet:

Boolean Operators & Modifiers

COMMAND	Google	Exalead	Bing	Duckduckgo
AND	Default	Default	Default	Default
OR	OR or the | (pipe) symbol	OR	OR or the | (pipe) symbol	OR
NOT	(minus sign) -	(minus sign) -	(minus sign) -	(minus sign) -
" "	"exact phrases"	"exact phrases"	"exact phrases"	"exact phrases"
*	Wildcard Search	N/A	N/A	N/A
( )	Not necessary	(resume OR cv)	(resume OR cv)	(resume OR cv)

Field Search Commands

COMMAND	Google	Exalead	Bing	Duckduckgo
Word in Title	intitle:	intitle:	intitle:	intitle:
Word in URL	inurl:	inurl:	N/A	N/A
Backlinks	N/A	link:	N/A	N/A
Xray	site:	site:	site:	site:
Number Range	98100..98999	N/A	N/A	N/A
FileType	filetype:xls	filetype:excel	filetype:xls	filetype:xls

How to find additional keywords for a search string:

To increase your chances of targeting the right lead candidate online, it's crucial to have a clear understanding of what you're searching for when creating a Boolean string. Researching additional keyword terms can significantly improve your chances of success. Fortunately, I've compiled a list of resources and tools to assist you in finding additional keyword suggestions.

When creating a Boolean string to find candidates online, it's important to search additional keywords for the search because it helps to ensure that the search string is comprehensive and specific enough to produce the desired results.

By adding additional keywords to the Boolean search string, you can increase the chances of finding candidates who meet your specific criteria. This is particularly important when searching for candidates in a highly competitive field or industry where there may be many other people with similar skills and qualifications. By including relevant keywords in the search string, you can filter out irrelevant or unrelated results, which can save you time and help you focus on the most promising candidates. Searching additional keywords for the Boolean search string can help you to create a more effective and efficient search that yields better results and saves you time and effort in the long run.

Resources:
There are several resources and tools available that can help you find additional search terms for job descriptions. Here are a few examples:

1. Job boards and aggregators:
Job boards like Indeed, Glassdoor, and Monster are excellent resources for finding additional search terms. You can search for similar job titles or browse job descriptions to identify relevant keywords.

2. Competitor job postings:
Looking at the job postings of your competitors can provide insight into the type of language and keywords they use to attract candidates.

3. LinkedIn and LinkedIn Insights:
LinkedIn is a great resource for finding additional search terms for job descriptions. You can search for similar job titles and

browse job descriptions to identify relevant keywords.

4. Thesaurus and Wikipedia:
Using a thesaurus can help you find synonyms for commonly used keywords in job descriptions, which can help you expand your search and find more relevant candidates.

5. Online glossaries:
These can be a great tool for finding relevant keywords related to your job search. By using these keywords in your job search, you can increase your chances of finding job listings that match your skills and experience.

6. Collocation dictionaries:
Can be a useful tool for language learners and writers who want to improve their understanding of how words are used in natural language. They can help writers avoid common mistakes and improve the fluency and naturalness of their writing by providing guidance on which words are most commonly used together.

7. Synonym dictionaries:

Can be very beneficial in finding additional terms related to a particular topic or concept. By expanding your vocabulary, identifying different shades of meaning, and improving the precision of your writing, you can become a more effective communicator and more knowledgeable on the topic at hand.

8. Iterations:

Are a useful strategy for finding alternative search terms related to a particular keyword or phrase.

Here's how you can use iterations to find additional search terms:

1. Start with your keyword: Begin with the keyword or phrase you want to find additional search terms for.

2. Make variations: Create variations of your keyword by changing the word order, using synonyms, adding prefixes or suffixes, or using different tenses. For example, if your keyword is "marketing manager," some iterations might include "manager of marketing," "marketing director," "digital marketing manager," or "brand marketing manager."

3. Use the iterations in your search: Once you have a list of iterations, use them in your search queries on job boards, search engines, and other job listing sites. This can help you find job listings that match your skills and experience, even if they don't use the exact same keywords as your original search.

4. Refine your iterations: If you're not getting the results you want, refine your iterations by testing different variations or using additional synonyms or related terms.

9. Misspelled words:
Misspelling words can sometimes be helpful when searching for candidates online, as it can help you find results that you might not have found otherwise. This can help improve your chances of finding neurodivergent professionals as well.

This is because people often make spelling mistakes when typing in their job titles or skills on their online profiles or resumes. For example, someone might misspell "administrative assistant" as "adminastrative assisstant". By misspelling a keyword in your search, you might uncover profiles or resumes that include the same misspelling.

Additionally, using common misspellings of a particular keyword can help you identify potential candidates who may not be using the correct spelling on their online profiles or resumes. This is particularly helpful when searching for candidates in highly competitive fields where there are many people with similar skills and qualifications.

10. Common words:
Searching common words may not necessarily help you find alternative words, as common words may have multiple meanings and be too broad to provide specific results. However, searching related words or synonyms of a common word can be a useful strategy for finding alternative words that are related to your search query.

 For example, if you're searching for job openings related to "writing," you might start by searching for common job titles such as "writer" or "copywriter." However, these terms may also bring up results that are not relevant to your search. To refine your search, you might try searching for related terms or synonyms such as "content creator," "communications specialist," or "content strategist."

Tools:
These tools can help you identify alternative search terms that can broaden your search and help you find more relevant results:

1. Chatgpt:
You can prompt ChatGPT to provide you with suggestions. Just let me know the job title you're interested in, and I'll offer some additional search terms to help you with your job search.

2. Glossary Tech:
This can be a valuable tool for finding additional keywords related to your job search. By using these keywords in your job search, you can increase your chances of finding job listings that match your skills and experience.

3. Keywordtool.io:
Can be used to find additional search terms related to your keyword or topic of interest. This can help you expand your search and find new opportunities for your business or personal interests.

4. Google's Keyword Planner:

Is a tool that can help you find additional search terms related to your target keywords.

Here's how you can use Google's Keyword Planner to find additional search terms:

1. Sign in to Google Ads: You need to have a Google Ads account to access Keyword Planner. If you don't have one, you can create a free account.

2. Access Keyword Planner: Once you're signed in to Google Ads, click on the "Tools & Settings" menu and select "Keyword Planner."

3. Enter your keyword: In the Keyword Planner, enter the keyword or phrase you want to find additional search terms for.

4. Review keyword ideas: Keyword Planner will provide you with a list of related keywords and their search volumes. Review the list to identify any relevant keywords that you may have missed.

5. Filter your results: You can filter the results by relevance, search volume, or other factors to help you find the most relevant keywords.

6. Export the results: If you want to keep a record of the keywords you've found, you can export the results to a spreadsheet or document.

Chapter 5: Boolean String Examples

In this chapter, we will combine what we learned from the previous chapters and create some completed search string examples.

First, we'll cover operator searches [OR, inurl, and intitle]. You can see how in the below screen shot on the string comes together.

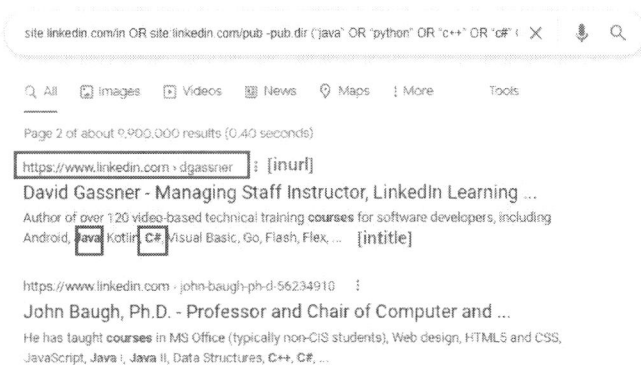

Natural Language Search
In layman's terms, semantic search seeks to understand natural language the way a human would. Using words and phrases that we expect to find within results helps us to find the right pages.

For example, try searching:

"Connect with me on LinkedIn"
"I am a veteran*"
"I graduated from the university of*"
"Earned my degree from*"

Try and factor this in when you are thinking about writing about Boolean strings.

Operator and Modifier Search Examples:

OR Search:

("for hire" OR "looking for a job" OR "searching for a job" OR "lost my job" OR "looking for new opportunities" OR "open to work" OR "open to new project")

Note: Make sure to use parentheses when using the OR operator.

site Searches:
site:com "cyber security" "our team" filetype:xlsx

site:ycombinator.com "who is hiring"

site inurl Searches:
site:com inurl:resume

site:edu inurl:directory

"What I'm doing with my life" "software engineer" inurl:profile

site intitle Searches:
site:com intitle:"about us"

site:com intitle:learn more here

intitle:"software|engineer|developer|programmer|architect" intitle:gmail.com

Asterisk Searches:
"contact me at **"

"email me * * @amazon.com"

Jonathan * Kidder@amazon.com

"has * engineering from university of minnesota"

site:meetup.com "software engineer at * *"

site:stackoverflow.com/cv"* * developer|engineer" (c rust OR c++ rust)

"prior to joining * *" "software developer|engineer"

"software developer|engineer"
intitle:"meet*team"

"* * developer|engineer" (c rust OR c++ rust)
inurl:resume -inurl:pdf

"I am * engineer | * developer at google" | "I
am * engineer | * developer at facebook" | "I
am * engineer | * developer at microsoft" | "I
am * engineer | * developer at ibm"

java|j2ee|c++ site:www.linkedin.com/in "*
power user with * *"|"* proficiency with * *"|"*
proficient with * *"|"* knowledge of|in|with *
"|" * yrs|years|experience of|in|with * *"|"*
expertise of|in|with * *"

site:"-*-" resume "developer|engineer" (c
rust OR c++ rust) -job|jobs *@gmail.com

"prior to joining * *" "software
developer|engineer"

Profile Searches:
(intitle:bio OR intitle:profile OR
intitle:homepage OR intitle:"about me")

(intitle:bio OR inurl:bio OR intitle:profile OR
inurl:profile OR intitle:homepage OR
inurl:homepage OR intitle:"about me" OR
inurl:"about me")

(intitle:bio OR intitle:profile OR intitle:follow me OR intitle:connect with me)

Resume Searches:
(inurl:resume OR intitle:resume) filetype:PDF

(intitle:resume OR intitle:cv) (filetype:pdf OR filetype:doc OR filetype:txt)

(resume OR cv) filetype:pdf

(intitle:resume OR inurl:resume OR intitle:cv OR inurl:cv OR intitle:vitae OR inurl:vitae)

(intitle:resume OR inurl:resume OR intitle:cv OR inurl:cv OR intitle:vitae OR inurl:vitae OR intitle:bio OR inurl:bio OR intitle:profile OR inurl:profile)

(intitle:resume OR inurl:resume OR intitle:bio OR inurl:bio OR intitle:vitae OR inurl:vitae OR intitle:cv OR inurl:cv OR intitle:homepage OR inurl:homepage)

"download my cv|resume" gmail.com

pdf|doc|docx gmail.com intitle:resume | inurl:resume

Event Searches:

(intitle:attendees OR inurl:attendees OR intitle:participants OR inurl:participants OR intitle:roster OR inurl:roster OR intitle:registrants OR inurl:registrants)

(intitle:*.attendee.list OR inurl:*.attendee.list OR insubject:*.attendee.list)
Directory Searches:

Directory Searches:
(members OR directory OR attendees)

(intitle:attendees OR inurl:attendees OR intitle:speakers OR inurl:speakers OR intitle:members OR inurl:members)
(intitle:team OR intitle:staff OR intitle:people OR intitle:employees)

(intitle:attendees OR intitle:members OR intitle:participants OR intitle:registrants OR intitle:roster)

(intitle:"staff directory" OR intitle:"employee directory" OR intitle:"member directory" OR intitle:"alumni directory")

inurl:meettheteam | inurl:meetourteam | inurl:leadershipteam | inurl:executiveteam | inurl:executiveleadership | inurl:"management team" | inurl:"our team" | inurl:"board members"

Alumni and College/University Searches:
(intitle:alumni OR intitle:graduates OR intitle:alum OR intitle:grads)

(intitle:grad OR inurl:grad)

Location Searches:
[Include the cities/towns within one search parentheses]

(richmond OR norfolk OR portsmouth OR hampton) (va OR virginia)

[Searching cities within a similar area]
("minneapolis" OR "saint paul" OR "golden valley")

[Searching Zip codes]
(55112 OR 55433 0R 55422 OR 554320)

Cell Number Searches:
"call me at * *"

("651*" OR "730*" OR "612*")

("contact me **" OR "reach me at *" OR "connect with *")

Email Address Searches:

(*@gmail.com OR *@msn.com OR *@yahoo.com)

("@dell.com" OR "@amazon.com" OR "@meta.com")

Facebook Searches:
site:facebook.com "Teacher" minneapolis inurl:people -pages

[Search for Specific Companies]
site:facebook.com "sales associate" minneapolis inurl:people -pages intitle:Target

LinkedIn Searches:

[The most basic foundational search is this]

site:linkedin.com/in OR site:linkedin.com/pub -pub.dir

[You can search hashtags]
site:Linkedin.com #opentowork

[Include a job title in your search]
site: linkedin.com/in OR site: linkedin.com/pub -pub.dir intitle:"Software Engineer"

site:www.linkedin.com/in "* worked with * at
* *" "software engineer|developer"

[Search for resume PDF's]
"software developer|engineer"
"linkedin|github" inurl:resume.pdf

[Search for candidates who work at a company]
site: linkedin.com/in OR
site:linkedin.com/pub -pub.dir
intitle:Amazon

[Search for locations (greater) expands the search for 50-mile radius]
site:www.linkedin.com/in OR
site:www.linkedin.com/pub -pub.dir
"greater minneapolis"

site:linkedin.com/in mongodb python sql
data modeling intitle:"san francisco bay
area"

[Search for languages]
site:linkedin.com/in OR
site:linkedin.com/pub -pub.dir Spanish
("native or bilingual proficiency")

[Search for gender perspective terms]

site:linkedin.com/in OR
site:linkedin.com/pub -pub.dir (her OR she)

site:www.linkedin.com/in "recommend her"
java|python aws|gcp|azure graphql|apollo

[Contact Me Search]
python spark "data engineer"
"email|contact me|at"
site:www.linkedin.com/in

gmail.com site:www.linkedin.com/in -
inurl:pub.dir
gmail.com site:www.linkedin.com "websites
* *
resume|cv|blog|personal|twitter|github|por
tfolio| stackoverflow|meetup"

Wordpress Searches:
site:wordpress.com/cv "Java Developer"

inurl:wp-content/uploads/2020 resume

inurl:wp-content/uploads/2020 attendees

inurl:wp-content/uploads member list

inurl:wp-content/uploads github
"gmail.com" intitle:resume OR inurl:resume
react redux

Reddit Searches:
site:reddit.com/user "veteran" ("about me" OR "personal website" OR "resume")

site:reddit.com/user "* * developer" "For Hire" Minneapolis

site:reddit.com/user ("* Engineer" OR "* Developer" OR "* Programmer") "remote work" ("about me" OR "personal website")

Facebook Searches:
site:facebook.com "software engineer" "Minneapolis" "to present" -posts

Craigslist Search:
site:*.craigslist.org/*/res account "Java Developer"

Twitter Searches:
site:twitter.com "engineer" "profile" "minneapolis"

site:twitter.com "Tweets and replies" -inurl:with_replies Software Engineer

site:twitter.com inurl:status "just start working at*"
site:twitter.com inurl:lists Engineers -inurl:members -inurl:subscribers

Sched Search:
site:sched.com/speaker/ "linkedin.com/in" "software engineer"

Beknown Search:
site:beknown.com "Java Developer"

Meetup Searches:
site:meetup.com/*/members -inurl:jobs -intitle:job

site:meetup.com inurl:member intitle:data.science

site:meetup.com (java OR python OR ruby OR C# OR C++) "member since"

site:meetup.com/software/members/ (java OR python OR ruby OR C# OR C++)

[Location searches]
site:meetup.com (java OR python OR ruby OR C# OR C++) 55110..554433 "member since"

site:meetup.com (java OR python OR rubyOR C# OR C++) intitle:"minneapolis" "member since"

[Network search]

site:meetup.com (java OR python OR rubyOR C# OR C++) "member since" "networks"

[Group event searches]
site:meetup.com "java" "meetups are scheduled"

site:meetup.com java intitle:MN meetups are scheduled

site:meetup.com "mobile" (kotlin OR android OR objective-c OR java) intitle:"minneapolis" "meetups are scheduled"

Kaggle Search:
site:kaggle.com "data scientist" "joined * ago" "united states"

Stack Overflow Searches:
site:careers.stackoverflow.com "web developer"

site:stackoverflow.com/users "software developer" "Minneapolis"

site:stackoverflow.com/cv "* * developer|engineer" (c rust OR c++ rust)

GitHub Searches:

[Basic search]
 site:github.com "joined github"
minneapolis "javascript"

site:github.com "block or report" full front
back "linkedin.com/in"

[Searching for email addresses]
site:github.com "joined github" minneapolis
"javascript" "*gmail.com"

[Searching for the most active users]
site:github.com "contributions in the last
year" minneapolis "javascript"

[Searching based on job titles]
site:github.com "joined on" "public activity"
-tab.activity "Java Developer" minneapolis

[Searching for Resumes]
(site:github.com OR site:github.io)
intitle:resume node mongodb

"resume|cv.tex at master * github" python

site:github.io/resume
(hadoop|hbase|nosql|foundationdb|orientd
b||arangodb|cortexdb|memacachedb|
couchdb|mongodb|BaseX|flockdb|stardog|i

nfinitydb|objectdb|RabbitMQ|DataDogHQ|"
* computing")

[Searching for LinkedIn users]
site:github.com followers following
"linkedin.com/in *" "rust|rustlang"
intitle:linkedin "https * github.com *"

GitHub.io Search:
site:github.io bitcoin "gmail.com"
"developer|engineer"

"hi|hello" "frontend|backend|fullstack"
"gmail.com" site:github.io

Polywork Search:
site:polywork.com "developer"

Gitlab Search:
site:gitlab.com "member since * *" python

Instagram Searches:
site:instagram.com "computer science" post
followers following

site:instagram.com "software developer"
(saint paul or minneapolis) -jobs -
inurl:company

site:instagram.com "UX designer"
(minneapolis or mn) -jobs -inurl:company

Google Drive Document Searches:

site:docs.google.com developer "San Francisco" intitle:resume -example -sample -samples -jobs
site:docs.google.com developer Atlanta (intitle:resume OR intitle:cv) -example -sample -samples -jobs

site:docs.google.com developer "San Francisco" (resume OR CV OR "curriculum vitae") -example -sample -samples -jobs

site:docs.google.com developer "* * @gmail.com" -example -sample -samples -jobs

site:docs.google.com "web|software developer|engineer" "gmail.com"

Google Spreadsheets:

site:docs.google/com/spreadsheets/ developer (contacts OR participants OR directory OR registrants OR attendees) -example

site:docs.google.com/spreadsheets/ Responses (contacts OR participants OR directory OR registrants OR attendees) -example

site:docs.google.com/spreadsheets/
Responses "email * * com|net|org" -example

site:docs.google.com/spreadsheets/ "List of
*" (contacts OR participants OR directory
OR registrants OR attendees) –example

Google Form Searches:
site:docs.google.com/spreadsheets/
Responses (contacts OR participants OR
directory OR registrants OR attendees) -
example

site:docs.google.com/spreadsheets/
Responses "email * * com|net|org" -example

site:docs.google.com/spreadsheets/ "List of
*" (contacts OR participants OR directory
OR
registrants OR attendees) –example

Google Presentation Searches:
site:docs.google.com/presentation/ docker -
example

site:docs.google.com/presentation/
"organizational chart" -example

Google Code Search:
site:https://code.google.com/u
inurl:gmail.com

Dev.to Searches:
site:dev.to intitle:dev.profile (data science OR scientist)

site:dev.to "joined on * *" "rust|rustlang"

Dev Post Search:
site:devpost.com intitle:software.portfolio.devpost

Dev Bistro Search:
site:devbistro.com/resumes inurl:gmail.com | inurl:yahoo.com | inurl:net | inurl:msn.com -keywords -india

Hacker Rack Searches:
site:hackerrank.com/profile (java OR ruby OR python OR c++)

site:hackerrank.com/profile (python sql OR python nosql)

Medium Searches:
site:medium.com/portfolio
site:medium.com (aws OR azure OR cloud architect) inurl:followers

site:medium.com "(useState()" OR "useEffect()" OR "unstated()" OR "useImperativeHandle()" OR "useLayoutEffect()" OR "useDebugValue()" OR "useContext()" OR "usereducer()"

CrunchBase Searches:
site:crunchbase.com/person react redux
site:crunchbase.com/person intitle:UX intitle:designer

Startup List Search:
site:startups-list.com/people

site:startups-list.com/people intitle:developer.talent

Stack Exchange Searches:
site:android.stackexchange.com/users
site:apple.stackexchange.com/users
site:bitcoin.stackexchange.com/users
site:codereview.stackexchange.com/users

YouTube Searches:
site:youtube.com "* is a * engineer"|"* is a * developer"|"is a * programmer" "rust"|"rustlang"

site:youtube.com/*/*/about "software engineer" "github|twitter"

site:youtube.com/*/*/about "I.am|m * web developer"

site:youtube.com/*/*/about "I.am|m *
software developer"

site:youtube.com/*/*/about "I.am|m *
software engineer"

Vimeo Search:
"location * * * * *" site:vimeo.com software
(engineer|developer|programmer|architect)
"joined * * ago"

Quora Search:
site:quora.com/profile software
(engineer|developer) "views * answers"

Xyz Search:
site:xyz "software engineer" "gmail.com"

Google Api:
site:*.googleapis.com/ (inurl:cv |
inurl:resume | inurl:vitae | intitle:resume) -
sample -format -"resume writer" -"resume
summary"

site:storage.googleapis.com/uxfolio/ inurl:cv

Uxfolio.io
site:uxfol.io/ inurl:contact

Chapter 6: Boolean Strings Including a Job Description

Once you've created the basic string the next step is to include job description search details. Since I primarily source for Software Engineers so I will walk through how I create a search. You can use the basics when creating strings for other industries. The foundation of it will be same.

Wikipedia defines a software engineer as a person who applies the principles of software engineering to the design, development, maintenance, testing, and evaluation of computer software.

A simple way to understand the difference between Front End and Back End in development is as follows:

Front End Languages: *HTML, CSS, Javascript*

Back End Languages: *Ruby, Python, Java, C, C#, C++, Javascript/Angular/React etc.*

Note: Use Stackshare to figure out a company's tech stack: site:stackshare.io/ inurl:my-stack
Once you understand the basics to the role the next step is to create a Boolean string. I've included a job description and highlight required and nice to have skills.

BASIC QUALIFICATIONS

· 4+ years of professional software development experience
· 3+ years of programming experience with at least one modern language such as Java, C++, or C# including object-oriented design
· 2+ years of experience contributing to the architecture and design (architecture, design patterns, reliability and scaling) of new and current systems
· Bachelor's degree in Computer Science or 8+ years of equivalent professional or military experience

PREFERRED QUALIFICATIONS

· Master's degree or relevant work experience
· 7+ years of professional experience in software development building production software systems
· Experience with AWS and other cloud technologies
· Experience taking a leading role in building complex software systems that have been successfully delivered to customers
· Knowledge of professional software engineering practices & best practices for the full software development life cycle, including coding standards, code reviews, source control management, build processes, testing, and operations
· Experience in communicating with users, other technical teams, and senior management to collect requirements, evaluate alternatives and describe product strategy, technical designs, and software product features
· Experience in full stack development ranging from front-end user interfaces through to back-end systems
· Experience working in an Agile/Scrum environment

It's also a good idea to conduct an intake meeting with your hiring manager to assess the preferred skills sets needed to perform the role.

Once you have a job description go through and highlight the basic skill requirements. From that point, search additional searchable terms.

You will add terms with AND OR NOT statements within your string. After reviewing additional terms and I started writing out examples below:

("object-oriented design" OR "ood" OR "design patterns" OR "design pattern" OR "software design") ("java" OR "python" OR "c++" OR "c#") AND ("system architecture" OR "distributed systems" OR "algorithms" OR "subversion" OR "software development" OR "software engineering")

("java" OR "python" OR "c++" OR "c#") ("system architecture" OR "distributed systems" OR "algorithms" OR "subversion") ("design patterns" OR "design pattern" OR "software design" OR "software development" OR "software engineering")

[Want to find graduates from these date suggestions]

("system architecture" OR "distributed systems" OR "algorithms" OR "data structure") ("design patterns" OR "design pattern" OR "software design" OR "software development" OR "software engineering" OR "system design") (2012 OR 2013 OR 2014 OR 2015 OR 2016 OR 2017)

("software engineer" OR "software developer" OR "developer" OR "engineer" OR "Software development engineer" OR "SWE" OR "MTS" OR "SDE") AND ("amazon" OR "google" OR "microsoft")

("java" OR "python" OR "c#" OR "c++") AND ("algorithms" OR "algorithm" OR "data structures" OR "data structure") ("software design" OR "software development" OR "software engineering") ("system architecture" OR "distributed systems" OR "distributed computing" OR "algorithms" OR "data Structure") ("software design" OR "software development" OR "software engineering" OR "system Design")

[I don't want to find managers or directors in my search]

("senior software engineer" OR "technical lead" OR "tech lead" OR "lead engineer" OR "lead developer" OR "senior lead" OR "principal Software engineer" OR "principle engineer" OR "senior engineer" OR "senior technical staff" OR "principal engineer") -manager –director -jobs -job -samples

("java" OR "python" OR "c++" OR "c#" OR "Ruby" OR "ood" OR "Programming") ("algorithm" OR "data structure" OR "algorithm" OR "Courses")

(software AND design* OR architect* OR develop* AND patent AND (services OR soa OR rest OR scale* OR mongo OR nosql OR soap) (java OR c# OR c++ OR python OR ruby OR groovy) (java or C# or C++ or python) AND ("developed" or "created" or "api" or "microservices") AND ("SDE" or "software engineer" or "software development engineer")

(java OR c++ OR c# OR python) (programmer OR engineer OR developer OR SDE) (algorithm OR "machine learning" OR "computer science*" OR problem*) (design* OR "object oriented" OR "object-oriented" OR soa OR "service oriented" OR "AWS" OR "Azure" OR "Rest" OR "web services" OR "service")

Notice how I did not try using job titles within my search? There will be so many variations from Software Developer to Software Engineer that I chose to only focus on the main requirements. You may need to do that in other industries as well.

Finally, combine the basic string and job description into one final string. This will take some experimenting because not all strings will give you good results. I've included some fully created strings below:

site:slideshare.net resume (java OR C# OR C++ OR python) ("developed" OR "created" OR "API" OR "microservices") ("SDE" OR "software engineer" OR "software development engineer")

site:docs.google.com engineer javascript

site:zoominfo.com/p/ "apple inc." "developer"

site:scribd.com (CV OR Vitae) "minneapolis" "developer"

site:polywork.com "developer" minneapolis

"* * developer|engineer" (c rust OR c++ rust) inurl:resume -inurl:pdf

(intitle:resume OR intitle:cv) ("software engineer" OR developer) (Java OR C++) -job -jobs -sample -examples site:com/cv OR site:com/resume "developer|engineer" (c rust OR c++ rust) -stackoverflow

inurl:resume.resume "software developer|engineer" "gmail.com"

site:linkedin.com/in OR site:linkedin.com/pub -pub.dir ("java" OR "python" OR "c++" OR "c#" OR "Ruby" OR "ood" OR "Programming") ("algorithm" OR "data structure" OR "algorithm" OR "Courses") -job -sample

Below I've included more Advanced Boolean string examples:

site:gdg.community.dev/u/ data engineering

site:com/author "software developer|engineer" "rust"

"* * developer|engineer" (c rust OR c++ rust) inurl:resume.pdf

site:stackoverflow.com/cv"* * developer|engineer" (c rust OR c++ rust) site:com/cv OR site:com/resume "developer|engineer" (c rust OR c++ rust) -stackoverflow

site:"-*-" resume "developer|engineer" (c rust OR c++ rust) -job|jobs "gmail.com"

site:github.com"rust" "Users who have contributed to this file"

site:gitcoin.co/profile

site:com/profile "software developer|engineer" nodejs|reactjs

related:github.io.resume "software developer|engineer" "gmail.com" -"ask hn"

"Amazon Web Services License AWS *" architect

"software developer|engineer" inurl:"meet*team"

"prior to joining * *" "software developer|engineer"

inurl:resume.resume "software developer|engineer" "gmail.com"

I encourage you to play around with these strings. Some may or may not fully work. You will have to make needed adjustments over time.

Chapter 7: Boolean Generator Tools

Boolean string searches are powerful, but they can seem tricky. These tools help simplify and auto generate Boolean strings with ease.

Why use Boolean Generator tools?
As a Recruiter, I'm constantly creating different Boolean strings for my searches. It's nice to have the option to use a generator tool to give additional suggestions when creating strings.

Note: Some of these generators still use [AND] in the search. If you are using Google, you can just remove that and add a [space] instead.

WebbTree
Rating: Beginner

Features:
• Basic and easy to understand
• Use job descriptions to auto fill in Boolean string examples
• Displays strings from all the major social media sites

• Store and save your favorite Boolean strings

WebbTree is a Boolean generator that will help any recruiter build better Boolean strings. Find quality talent using our free Boolean search string builder.

Here's how it works. Simply log into Webbtree and create a free account.

To start using the tool, follow the very simple to use format and enter the keywords. In this example, we're looking for a "Software Engineer" who has coded in "Java" and lives in the "Greater Minneapolis-St. Paul, MN" market.

Sites include LinkedIn, Facebook, Twitter, GitHub, Stack Overflow, Xing, Viadeo, Behance, Elance, and UpWork, About.me, Pinterest, Weibo, & Kaggle.

Hiretual (HireEZ) "Boolean Generator"
Rating: Beginner

Features:
• Use job descriptions or other skill set requirements and it will auto create a string.

• It has a large database of additional job title and search terms suggestions

Hiretual has a great internal Boolean generator within its platform. To begin your search, click on the Toolbox. From there, you can choose relevant job titles, skills, industry, and location and create Boolean search strings based on them. Then you can select any of the platforms on which to search.

They are divided into the most popular, generic platforms, Healthcare, Designers and Research, Mechanica, Games, and Others. After that, you click Search Talent Now, and your results will be visible in the next tab. Hiretual is a capable recruiting CRM system. Great Facebook search tool and integration with portals like GitHub and Stack Overflow make it a market leader in my opinion.

Recruitin.net
Rating: Beginner

Features:
· A clean new interface
· Job title suggestions as you type
· Much faster loading
· Search LinkedIn by employer

The tool gives you keywords that help your job ads rank in Google, Indeed and job boards and ensure they resonate with candidates you're looking for. The more you use it, the better it gets. There's nothing else like it and it's still free and anonymous.

This tool is a simple way to construct the very same Boolean queries (and more), but with the benefit of a nice simple interface.

It's entirely free and anonymous and not in any way shape or form associated with LinkedIn, which is a registered trademark of the LinkedIn Corporation.

Recruit'em (formerly RecruitIn before LinkedIn's lawyers strenuously objected) is a project by Clever Biscuit, a 5 professional computer types who build free tools to help people out. Also, this tool has awesome integration in different platforms, like:

- LinkedIn
- Dribbble
- GitHub
- Xing
- Stack Overflow
- Twitter

BooleanAssistant
Rating: Beginner

Features:
Has a large library of Boolean string examples.
· Connect APIs to automate tasks
· Great for non-technical users

BooleanAssistant, a boolean generator and email hunter. BooleanAssistant is your best recruiting and sourcing assistant to generate boolean search strings and find people's emails.

This chrome extension is free to use and installing it is such a simple process. Just go on Google and type the BooleanAssistant. Then just with one click install this tool and start using it. It is focused on LinkedIn for finding candidates there and automating other recruiting tasks no matter your ability to use technologies for different purposes.

Bool
Rating: Beginner

Features:
· Quickly build and launch Boolean searches
· Create and save strings
· Keeps you organized

• Easy to use

This free extension helps create strings and saves them in one convenient place. It's called BOOL (Boolean Search Assistant). It has 4,000 active users and is highly rated by its users. With that in mind, I wanted to do a review of this extension tool.

BOOL is a chrome extension that streamlines Boolean string construction and x-ray search. The first version was launched in 2016 and has since gone through several iterations. From features such as page analysis and Boolean String Bank integration, the core functionalities have been distilled for greater effectiveness as a search tool.

Whether you are building a target list of companies, titles or skills, BOOL allows you to conveniently and quickly build Boolean strings and launch searches from any window.

How to Use Bool:
1. Build a Boolean table of AND (blue), OR (green), and NOT (red) rows/columns by clicking the respective buttons.

2. Populate the Boolean table by grouping similar search criteria into the same columns. Add the required criteria to the blue and green rows (AND and OR) and those not required to the red rows (NOT).
3. Choose the desired search engine, website (for X-ray searches), or filetype (pdf, doc, docx, ppt, or xls).
4. Your Boolean string is built instantly.
5. Quickly run that string search on Google or Bing.
6. Finally, save your search string to the clipboard.

BOOL will continue to evolve as more user-friendly and efficient methods are integrated within the platform. Take the time to write a review in the chrome store about this tool. The Bool team really appreciates any feedback or thoughts on the tool's functionality.

Conclusion

I hope you've gained insights on Boolean strings and have found value from these chapters. During the pandemic writing has filled my home with excitement and warmth. It has helped me to revitalize my passions within my field.

I've written on several topics within recruiting and have received so many kind notes and messages from recruiters across the world. I can't thank you enough for that. It has enlightened and humbled me greatly.

If you have a few minutes to spare, would you consider leaving an honest review of this book on Amazon? I believe that many recruiters could benefit from its insights, and your review could help others decide if it's right for them. The book covers the fundamentals of a Boolean string, so there's no need to pay for expensive courses to learn this important skill. Thank you for your time!

Resources:

Boolean Operator	Purpose	Example Boolean Search Strings
AND	Locates resources that contain two or more keywords	Developer AND Python
OR	Locates resources that contain at least one of a list of two or more keywords	Developer OR Engineer OR Programmer
NOT	Excludes resources that contain a keyword	Python NOT snake, Python - Monty
" " (quotation marks)	Locates resources that contain an exact phrase	"Data Infrastructure Engineer"

site:	Locates resources on a particular website	Blockchain software engineer site:twitter.com
inurl:	Locates resources that contain one or more keyword(s) in the URL	inurl:resume

Most Common Tech Roles:

Role / Specialization	Example Boolean String
Java Developer	(developer OR SDE OR engineer OR programmer OR MTS OR "member of technical staff") AND Java AND (Spring OR JSF OR Hibernate OR Struts OR Play OR Grails)
Python Developer	(developer OR SDE OR engineer OR programmer OR MTS OR "member of technical

	staff") AND Python AND (Django OR Flask)
Frontend (UI/UX)	UI OR UX OR "user interface" OR "user experience" OR designer
Backend (Application)	(application OR API OR microservices OR "server side") AND (Python OR Ruby OR Java OR GO OR Node OR Scala OR C OR C++ OR C#) AND (Spring OR Rails OR Django OR Flask)
Frontend (Application)	JavaScript AND (React OR Angular OR Vue)
Full stack (Application)	(Python OR Ruby OR Java OR GO OR Node OR Scala OR C OR C++ OR C# OR Spring OR Rails OR Django OR Flask) AND (React OR Angular OR Vue)

Infrastructure or Platform (Cloud)	("distributed systems" OR "cloud infrastructure" OR "cloud infra" OR ("cloud and infrastructure) OR "infrastructure as a service" OR IAAS OR (cloud AND platform) OR (AWS OR "Amazon Web Services" OR Azure OR GCP OR "Google Cloud Platform") AND (Docker OR Kubernetes OR Jenkins OR Salt OR Ansible OR Puppet OR Chef OR Terraform)
Infrastructure (Data)	("data infrastructure" OR "data infra" OR "data architecture" OR "distributed systems" OR "data processing" OR framework OR "big data") AND (Hadoop OR Spark OR Kafka OR Flink OR Storm)
DevOps / SRE	DevOps OR SRE OR "site reliability" AND (Python OR Ruby OR Java OR GO OR Node OR Scala OR C OR C++ OR C#) AND (Docker OR Kubernetes OR Ansible OR Chef OR Puppet OR Salt OR Terraform) AND (AWS OR "Amazon Web Services" OR

	Azure OR GCP OR "Google Cloud Platform")
Data / ETL	("Data engineer" OR "extract transform and load" OR ETL OR "data pipelines" OR "data ingestion" OR "data processing") AND (Python OR Scala OR Java)
Data Warehouse Engineer	SQL AND (Bash or Python or scripting) AND ("business intelligence" OR SAS OR Tableau) AND ("data warehouse" OR "data warehousing" OR Redshift OR Snowflake OR Oracle)
Machine Learning	(Python OR Scala OR Java) AND (Scikit-learn OR TensorFlow OR Pytorch OR Keras OR "machine learning" OR ML)
Embedded	(embedded OR "low level" OR hardware OR firmware) AND (C OR C++)

Security	(Python OR Go OR Java OR Node OR C or C++) AND (AWS OR Azure OR GCP OR Docker OR Kubernetes) OR (security OR TCP/IP OR firewalls OR Okta OR CyberArk OR Proofpoint OR Tanium)
Game	C# OR C++ AND (Unity OR Unity32 OR Unreal OR Open3d OR game)
Mobile	(developer OR engineer OR programmer) AND (mobile OR Android OR iOS OR Objective-C OR Swift OR Cocoa OR Cocoa-Touch OR SwiftUI OR XCode)
QA	(tester OR QA OR "quality assurance" OR SDET OR "software development engineer in test" OR "test automation" OR "automation tester" OR "automation engineer")

Individual Contributor	developer OR SDE OR engineer OR programmer OR MTS OR "member of technical staff" NOT (manager OR head OR director OR VP OR founder

Boolean FAQ:

What is a Boolean string?

A Boolean string is a string that contains one or more Boolean operators (AND, OR, NOT) and is used to evaluate logical expressions.

What are Boolean operators?

Boolean operators are logical operators used to combine or manipulate Boolean values. They include AND, OR, and NOT.

How do you use a Boolean string?

To use a Boolean string, you first need to understand the logic of the expression you are trying to evaluate. You can then use the appropriate Boolean operators to combine or manipulate Boolean values to get the desired result.

What is the difference between AND OR operators?

The AND operator returns true only if both operands are true, while the OR operator returns true if at least one of the operands is true.

What is the NOT operator?

The NOT operator is a unary operator that returns the opposite of a Boolean value. If the value is true, NOT returns false, and if the value is false, NOT returns true.

What is the order of precedence for Boolean operators?

The order of precedence for Boolean operators is NOT, AND, and then OR. However, it's always best to use parentheses to clarify the order of evaluation.

Can you use Boolean strings in programming languages?

Yes, Boolean strings are commonly used in programming languages to evaluate logical expressions and make decisions based on the result.

What are some common mistakes to avoid when using Boolean strings? Common mistakes include forgetting to use parentheses to clarify the order of evaluation, using the wrong operator, and not understanding the logic of the expression you are trying to evaluate.

Is a Boolean search operator case-sensitive? Answer: Yes, Boolean operators (AND, NOT, OR) are case-sensitive. However, keywords are not case-sensitive. For example, "Python AND Spark" is different from "Python and Spark." But "Python AND Spark" is the same as "python AND spark."

What is the difference between Boolean Searching and Advanced Search? Answer: Boolean searching involves using Boolean operators to specify the relationships between different terms in a search query to generate search results. On the other hand, advanced search utilizes filters and

search criteria to generate search results.
Advanced search is a feature provided by
specific search engines and may vary from
engine to engine.

WIZARD SOURCER

Please follow WizardSourcer.com for my
latest updates.

Printed in Great Britain
by Amazon